It Should Be Thrown With Great Force

It Should Be Thrown with Great Force

Practical Advice for Working Writers:
A Compendium of Notes, Quotes, and Anecdotes

Edited by Tim Hensley

Little Fox Press
BRISTOL, VIRGINIA

Copyright © 2015 by Tim Hensley

All rights reserved. No part of this publication may be reproduced or transmitted in any form or by any means, electronic or mechanical, including photocopy, recording, or any information storage and retrieval system, without the prior written permission of the publisher, except in the case of brief quotations embodied in critical reviews and certain other noncommercial uses permitted by copyright law.

Little Fox Press
818 Cumberland Street
Bristol, VA 24201

This is a work of non-fiction. Cover art by Mr. Hensley's essay class.

Ordering information is available at www.littlefoxpress.com
It Should Be Thrown With Great Force / Tim Hensley. — 1st ed.
ISBN 978-0-9861880-1-5

Contents

Preface 13

First Principles 15

Truth 22

Learning the Craft 24

The Reader 28

Getting Started 31

Voice 35

Style 39

Simplicity 45

Language 49

Beginnings 57

Endings 60

Revision 62

Editors 67

Money 70

The Writing Life 72

Critics and Criticism 83

A Sample Query Letter 87

The Elements of Lincoln's Grammar 90

17 Figures of Speech 97

The Anglo-Saxon Element 103

The Cumulative Sentence 115

To my old professor,
L. Percival Breusch

It's true that most books for beginning writers are not very good, even those written with the best of intentions, and no doubt this one, like others, will have its faults.

—JOHN GARDNER

Preface

ANYONE WHO SETS OUT TO WRITE FOR PUBLICATION will soon discover the plethora of instructional materials available to writers. There are, in fact, so many helps on the market—books, magazines, on-line courses, MFA programs, even shirts and mugs for writers—that it would be easy to cast the people behind these aids as professional wannabes: "Those who can write; those who can't teach English."

My own experience counsels otherwise. If space allowed, I could tell of books and articles that have given my writing (or my understanding of the publishing process) a much needed lift. Often this help has come in the form of a quote that encapsulates what I have been learning by trial and error but have never put into words.

Over the years I have collected these quotes in file folders, on scraps of paper, in books and magazines marked with sticky notes. They are the bits of writing wisdom I return to time and again. I bring them together here for the edification of budding scribes.

Tim Hensley
August 2015

{ 1 }

First Principles

Write the vision and make it plain.

HABAKKUK 2:2

Every prudent man dealeth with knowledge.

PROVERBS 13:16

Write about what really interests you, whether it is real things or imaginary things, and nothing else. (Notice this means that if you are interested only in writing you will never be a writer, because you will have nothing to write about.)

C.S. LEWIS

The preacher sought to find pleasing words, and uprightly he wrote the words of truth.

ECCLESIASTES 12:10

The real novelist, the one with an instinct for what he is about, knows that he cannot approach the infinite directly, that he must penetrate the natural human world as it is.

FLANNARY O'CONNOR

The storyteller's primary job in narration is to "exercise power" over the reader to make him want to listen.

JULIE CHECKOWAY

The writer, always revealing, is known intimately to his reader, who remains to him a perfect stranger.

T. HENSLEY

And with many parables spake he the word unto them, as they were able to hear it. But without a parable spake he not unto them.

MARK 4:33-34A

A writer cannot be wise enough to be a great artist without being wise enough to be a philosopher. A writer cannot have the energy to produce good art without having the energy to wish to pass beyond it. A small artist is content with art; a great artist is content with nothing except everything.

G.K. CHESTERTON

Of making many books there is no end.

ECCLESIASTES 12:12B

A scrupulous writer, in every sentence that he writes, will ask himself at least four questions, thus: 1. What am I trying to say? 2. What words will express it? 3. What image or idiom will make it clearer? 4. Is this image fresh enough to have an effect?

GEORGE ORWELL

The reason why so few good books are written is that so few people who can write know anything.

WALTER BAGEHOT

There is no such thing as an artist: there is only the world, lit or unlit as the light allows. When the candle is burning, who looks at the wick? When the candle is out, who needs it? But the world without light is wasteland and chaos, and a life without sacrifice is abomination.

ANNIE DILLARD

If I discover within myself a desire which no experience in this world can satisfy, the most probable explanation is that I was made for another world.

C.S. LEWIS

The point of an open mind, like having an open mouth, is to close it on something solid.

G.K. CHESTERTON

As soon as beauty is sought not from religion and love, but for pleasure, it degrades the seeker.

ANNIE DILLARD

Sweet are the uses of adversity,
Which like the toad, ugly and venomous,
Wears yet a precious jewel in his head;
And this life, exempt from public haunt,
Finds tongues in trees, books in running brooks,
Sermons in stones, and good in everything.

WILLIAM SHAKESPEARE

Death and life are in the power of the tongue, and they that love it shall eat the fruit thereof.

PROVERBS 18:21

When words are many sin is not lacking.

PROVERBS 10:19

He that hath knowledge spareth his words; and a man of understanding is of an excellent spirit.

PROVERBS 17:27

Brevity is the soul of wit.

WILLIAM SHAKESPEARE

A story can only have one fault: that of making the audience not want to know what happens next.

E.M. FORSTER

Beneath the rule of men entirely great,
The pen is mightier than the sword.

EDWARD BULWER-LYTTON

The skill of writing is to create a context in which other people can think.

EDWIN SCHLOSSBERG

How vain it is to sit down to write when you have not stood up to live.

HENRY DAVID THOREAU

At the heart of every good plot is a protagonist who wants something very badly, and runs into all sorts of troubles and reversals trying to get it.

T. HENSLEY

Be generous, be delicate, and always pursue the prize.

HENRY JAMES

Good fiction tells us what we know, but don't quite know that we know.

WALKER PERCY

In reading books and making arguments, the point is not to change the world, but to understand it.

KEN MYERS

There is only one way to defeat the enemy, and that is to write as well as one can. The best argument is an undeniably good book.

SAUL BELLOW

A book must be the axe for the frozen sea within us.

FRANZ KAFKA

A writer should write what he has to say and not speak it.

ERNEST HEMINGWAY

When you write your object is to convey every sensation, sight, feeling, emotion, to the reader…when you walk into a room and you get a certain feeling or emotion, remember back until you see exactly what it was that gave you the emotion. Remember what the noises and smells were and what was said. Then write it down, making it clear so the reader will see it too and have the same feeling you had. And watch people, observe, try to put yourself in somebody else's head. If two men argue, don't just think who is right and who is wrong. Think what both their sides are. As a man, you know who is right and who is wrong; you have to judge. As a writer, you should not judge, you should understand.

ERNEST HEMINGWAY

Preaching is the art not of browbeating, but of persuading, in a way that shows both respect for the human mind and reverence for the God who made it. Christian persuasion requires wisdom, love patience, and holy humanness. It is a fine art as well as a useful one, and it becomes for preachers a lifetime study, concern, and challenge.

J.I. PACKER

If you want to write essays, you need two ingredients: a few topics you've thought deeply about, and some ability to ferret out the unexpected. What should you think about? My guess is that it doesn't matter—that anything can be interesting if you get deeply enough into it.

PAUL GRAHAM, "THE AGE OF THE ESSAY"

Your pieces are filled with interesting, specific information; they have a clear focus; they are well written; but they are not likely to be published without revision. [Why?]...They do not have an urgency, a significance, an unexpectedness, a tension that will draw in a reader who is not already fascinated by your subject.

DONALD MURRAY

Essay (n.) 1590s, "trial, attempt, endeavor," also "short, discursive literary composition" (first attested in writings of Francis Bacon, probably in imitation of Montaigne), from Middle French *essai* "trial, attempt, essay" (in Old French from 12c.), from Late Latin *exagium* "a weighing, a weight," from Latin *exigere* "drive out; require, exact; examine, try, test," from *ex-* "out" (see ex-) + *agere* (see act (n.)) apparently meaning here "to weigh." The suggestion is of unpolished writing.

Essay (v.) "to put to proof, test the mettle of," late 15c., from Middle French *essaier*, from *essai* "trial, attempt" (see **essay** (n.)). This sense has mostly gone with the divergent spelling *assay*. Meaning "to attempt" is from 1640s.

ONLINE DICTIONARY OF WORD ETYMOLOGIES

The art of writing has for backbone some fierce attachment to an idea.

VIRGINIA WOOLF

Good writing takes place at intersections, at what you might call knots, at places where the society is snarled or knotted up.

MARGARET ATWOOD

{ 2 }

Truth

Speak the truth in love.

EPHESIANS 4:15

There are few nudities so objectionable as the naked truth.

AGNES REPPLIER

Truth is so excellent that if it but praises small things, they become noble.

LEONARDO DA VINCI

Truth is like a lion; all you need to do is let it out of the cage.

C.S. LEWIS

And ye shall know the truth, and the truth shall make you free.

JOHN 8:32

Truth is a river that is sober and slow / And tears will be washed to the sea.

MARK HEARD

Men occasionally stumble over the truth, but most of them pick themselves up and hurry off as if nothing happened.
Sir Winston Churchill

The louder he talked of his honor, the faster we counted our spoons.
Ralph Waldo Emerson

We know the truth not only by reason, but also by the heart.
Blaise Pascal

The recent evolution of the English novel suggests that truth was once too pressing to be played at.
T. Hensley

When we understand the outside of things, we think we have them. Yet the Lord puts his things in sub-defined, suggestive shapes, yielding no satisfactory meaning to the mere intellect, but unfolding themselves to the conscience and heart.
George MacDonald

The truth must dazzle gradually.
Emily Dickinson

Questioning ourselves and our world, finding in it, for all its coincidence, accidents, and contingencies a mysterious coherence, we may become aware of a horizon beyond which abides the One who is the creator and context of our existence.
Ron Hansen

… { 3 }

Learning the Craft

Reading maketh a full man, conference a ready man, and writing an exact man.
Francis Bacon

Read all the good books you can, and avoid nearly all magazines.
C.S. Lewis

I never desire to converse with a man who has written more than he has read.
Samuel Johnson

All originality and no plagiarism makes for dull preaching.
C.H. Spurgeon

I would not know how to advise a man how to write. It is a matter of talent and interest. I believe he must be strongly moved if he is to become a writer. Writing is like a "lust," or like "scratching when you itch." Writing comes as a result of a very strong impulse, and when it does come, I for one must get it out.

C.S. Lewis

Everywhere I go I'm asked if I think the universities stifle writers. My opinion is that they don't stifle enough of them. There's many a best-seller that could have been prevented by a good teacher.

Flannary O'Connor

Learning to be a writer seemed to me from the outset to be an impossible pursuit, one for which I had no preparation or training, or even motive, except for a secret and undeniable urge to do so.

Alice McDermott

You can't teach people to write well. Writing is something God lets you do or declines to let you do.

Kurt Vonnegut

Whether you use a fountain pen or a word processor, writing is finally sitting alone in a room and wrenching it out of yourself, and nobody can teach you that.

Jon Winokur

Learn to handle the English language. The best help for this is Strunk: *The Elements of Style*, a perfect gem of a little book, indispensable for all of us.

Elisabeth Elliot

Every writer seeks out style and the equally elusive "voice." Too often, the path leads to the wrong places, the most notable of the wrong places being the soul-deadening (and pen dulling)...*Elements of Style* by E.B. White and William Strunk.

ALEX BEAM

After I had separated from my father, I studied English grammar, imperfectly of course, but so as to speak and write as well as I do now.

ABRAHAM LINCOLN

If you, like many a misguided youth are under the impression that the study of grammar is dry and irksome, and a matter of little consequence, I trust I shall succeed in removing from your mind, all such false notions and ungrounded prejudices; for I will endeavor to convince you, before I close these lectures, that this is not only a pleasing study, but one of real and substantial utility; a study that directly tends to adorn and dignify human nature, and meliorate the condition of man...Nothing of a secular nature can be more worthy of your attention, then, than the acquisition of grammatical knowledge.

SAMUEL KIRKHAM

Writing at its best, is a lonely life. Organizations for writers palliate the writer's loneliness, but I doubt if they improve his writing.

ERNEST HEMINGWAY

Fortune favors the prepared mind.

LOUIS PASTEUR

If you don't have the time to read, you don't have the time or the tools to write.

STEPHEN KING

This class is meant to acquaint you with the literary and rhetorical tradition of the essay, a genre which has been described as "the meeting ground between art and philosophy" and by another as "the place where the self finds a pattern in the world, and the world finds a pattern in the self."

ANTHONY LIOI

In those years I taught Rhetoric. Overcome myself by the desire of money, I offered for sale skill in speech to overcome others by.

SAINT AUGUSTINE

No assemblage of writing proverbs can replace such classic travel guides as Strunk and White's *Elements of Style* or William Zinsser's *On Writing Well*; they can serve as a kind of road map for the writer who is already in motion.

T. HENSLEY

Nowadays authors are coached on "building your brand" more than on improving their writing. Publishers care more about website stats and Twitter followers than the quality of an author's work.

PHILIP YANCEY

There are three rules for writing a novel. Unfortunately no one knows what they are.

W. SOMERSET MAUGHAM

{4}

The Reader

Why should you examine your writing style with the idea of improving it? Do so as a mark of respect for your readers, whatever you're writing. If you scribble your thoughts any which way, your readers will surely feel that you care nothing about them. They will mark you down as an egomaniac or a chowderhead—or worse, they will stop reading you.

KURT VONNEGUT

The main thing I try to do is write as clearly as I can. Because I have the greatest respect for the reader, and if he's going to the trouble of reading what I've written—why, the least I can do is make it as easy as possible for him to find out what I'm trying to say, trying to get at. I rewrite a good deal to make it clear.

E.B. WHITE

I sometimes think that writing is like driving sheep down a road. If there is any gate open to the left or the right, the readers will most certainly go into it.

C.S. LEWIS

Take the reader into your confidence, rather than seeing him as an opponent.

ROGER ANGELL

We never know how much has been missing from our lives until a true writer comes along.

ALFRED KAZIN

Writing books that appear only in Christian bookstores only to be read by church people requires little cunning; writing books of faith for a readership that has only vestigial organs of perception—that requires a particular kind of shrewdness.

PHILLIP YANCEY

Sir, do you read a book through?

SAMUEL JOHNSON

If a writer wrote merely for his time, I would have to break my pen and throw it away.

VICTOR HUGO

Successful authors write to their readers as though they know them.

KENNETH HENSON

I write for those who judge of books, not by the quantity, but by the quality of them: who ask not how long, but how good are they?

I spare both my reader's time and my own, by couching my sense in as few words as I can.

JOHN WESLEY

Good writing works from a simple premise: Your experience is not yours alone, but in some sense a metaphor for everyone's.

KIM ADDONOZIO

{5}

Getting Started

In creating, the only hard thing's to begin; / A grass blade's no easier to make than an oak.

JAMES RUSSEL LOWELL

A writer will do anything to avoid the act of writing. I can testify from my newspaper days that the number of trips made to the water cooler per reporter hour far exceeds the body's known need for fluid.

WILLIAM ZINSSER

Writing is easy. All you do is sit staring at a blank sheet of paper until drops of blood form on your forehead.

RED SMITH

Don't talk away your story or article before, or instead of, writing it.

JUDY DELTON

A man may write at any time, if he will set himself doggedly to it.
SAMUEL JOHNSON

Ernest Hemingway got up at first light, and from 5:00 A.M. to 10:00 A.M., he wrote standing up, shifting his weight from foot to foot. Only when the writing was flowing well did he move to a typewriter and a chair.
SOPHY BURNAM

A woman must have money and a room of her own if she is to write fiction.
VIRGINIA WOLF

Appealing workplaces are to be avoided. One wants a room with no view, so imagination can meet memory in the dark.
ANNIE DILLARD

It is seldom possible to gauge beforehand what will prove a fruitful topic or which anecdote will fire the imagination. Some matters move us, some do not. The writer gleans wind scraps; he listens wherever he can.
NICHOLAS DELBANCO

A man would do well to carry a pencil in his pocket, and write down the thoughts of the moment. Those that come unsought are generally the most valuable, and should be secured because they seldom return.
FRANCIS BACON

If you leave a sentence incomplete or a thought half finished, you can pick up the next morning's work more quickly.

SOPHY BURNHAM

We do not write because we want to; we write because we have to.

W. SOMERSET MAUGHAM

Advice to writers: Sometimes you just have to stop writing. Even before you begin.

STANISLAW J. LEC

If it's interesting to me, and I haven't seen a dozen columns about it, then it's probably pretty good stuff. Ninety percent of my job is thinking things through and deciding how I feel about an event, a person, or whatever.

RHETA GRIMSLEY JOHNSON

A writer who waits for ideal conditions under which to work will die without putting a word to paper.

E.B. WHITE

The important thing is to work every day. I work from about seven until about noon. Then I go fishing of swimming, or whatever I want. The best way is always to stop when you are going good. If you do that you'll never be stuck. And don't think or worry about it until you start to write again the next day. That way your subconscious will be working on it all the time, but if you worry about it, your brain will get tired before you start again. But work every day. No matter what has happened the day or night before, get up and bite on the nail.

ERNEST HEMINGWAY

Writing comes more easily if you have something to say.

SHOLEM ASCH

A word about the process of gathering material. A writer's "field" is the whole universe. Everywhere you go, everything you do or see, is the raw material. Make notes. As you find yourself thinking more and more about a particular subject, drop the notes into file folders labeled with broad topics. One of these days that folder may turn into a book, or before you tackle a book, why not have a go at an article for your local paper, church paper, or a magazine?

ELIZABETH ELLIOT

Gibbon's early studies, pursued at home until he was sixteen because he was frail and ill, were encouraged by...his aunt. He spent most of his time at the Oxford University library in desultory reading. Fortunately, during a residence in Switzerland from 1753 to 1758, Daniel Pavillard taught Gibbon how to study systematically.

EARLE E. CAIRNES

{6}

Voice

Writing is both an art and a craft and you can learn by doing it. To see things you want to say, and to have ideas about how to say them, is how it starts: then you have to find the sound of your own voice talking on paper, and you can only do that by reading your initial drafts and making improvements. It is as simple—and as difficult—as that.

J.I. PACKER

Most that is first written on any subject is mere groping after it, mere rubble stone and foundation.

HENRY DAVID THOREAU

Writing became such a process of discovery that I couldn't wait to get to work in the morning to see what I was going to say.

SHARON OBRIEN

Always write (and read) with the ear, not the eye. You should hear every sentence you write as if it was being read aloud or spoken. If it does not sound nice, try again.

C.S. Lewis

The question of ear is vital. Only the writer whose ear is reliable is in a position to use bad grammar deliberately; only he knows for sure when a colloquialism is better than formal phrasing; only he is able to sustain his work at the level of good taste. So cock your ear.

E.B. White

Creativity is a by-product of hard work. If I never have another really new idea, it won't matter.

Andy Rooney

Even in literature and art, no man who bothers about originality will ever be original: whereas if you simply try to tell the truth (without caring two pence how often it has been told before) you will, nine times out of ten, become original without ever having noticed it.

C. S. Lewis

A classic is classic not because it conforms to certain structural rules, or fits certain definitions (of which its author had quite probably never heard). It is classic because of a certain eternal and irrepressible freshness.

Edith Wharton

The man who writes about himself and his own time is the only man who writes about all people and all time.

George Bernard Shaw

See things as they are and write about them. Don't waste your creative energy trying to make things up. Even if you are writing fiction, write the things you see and know.

REAL LIVE PREACHER.COM

This is the challenge of writing. You have to be very emotionally engaged in what you're doing, or it comes out flat. You can't fake your way through this.

REALLIVEPREACHER.COM

The key to non-anxious sermon-writing is that it's not about me. It's about the congregation. I honor the fact that the listeners bring more to the sermon than I do. I remind myself of the hundreds of times someone says, 'I loved how you said…' and then tell me things that they heard that were nowhere in my text and that I never said. But they heard what they needed to hear.

REVEREND SEAN PARKER DENNISON

Explosions of human creativity are unthinkable apart from the unconscious. Poetry is our unconscious connections of pictures, words, sounds and meanings leaking out to consciousness line by line. Even the grueling process of revision, the overtly conscious effort to make a poem better, may simply be an attempt to orient the material more accurately to the voice one hears faintly within. This may explain why a piece of poetry or prose requires many drafts before it sounds like the author's voice.

DAVID HANSON

Aim at authenticity, NEVER at style, originality, or "creativity."

ELISABETH ELLIOT

Your manuscript is both good and original, but the part that is good is not original and the part that is original is not good.
>   ATTRIBUTED TO SAMUEL JOHNSON

I would not have been a poet / except that I have been in love / alive in this mortal world.
>   WENDELL BERRY

Fondness for material you've gone to a lot of trouble to gather isn't a good enough reason to include it if it's not central to the story you've chosen to tell. Self-discipline bordering on masochism is required. The only consolation for the loss of so much material is that it isn't totally lost; it remains in your writing as an intangible that the reader can sense. Readers should always feel that you know more about your subject than you've put into writing.
>   WILLIAM ZINSSER

Most writing touches the divine spirit only glancingly; we are too full our own opinions, or of the desire to be appreciated.
>   T.HENSLEY

Style

{7}

If I broke all the rules of punctuation, had words mean whatever I wanted them to mean, and strung them together higgledy-piggledy, I would simply not be understood. So you too better avoid Picasso-style or jazz-style writing, if you have something worth saying and want to be understood.

KURT VONNEGUT

A careful and honest writer does not need to worry about style. As he becomes proficient in the use of the language, his style will emerge, because he himself will emerge, and when this happens he will find it increasingly easy to break through the barriers that separate him from other minds, other hearts—which is, of course, the purpose of writing, as well as its principal reward.

E.B. WHITE

I've always felt that my "style"—the careful projection onto paper of who I think I am—was my only marketable asset, the only possession that might set me apart from other writers. Therefore

I've never wanted anyone to fiddle with it, and after I submit an article I protect it fiercely.

WILLIAM ZINSSER

The great authors share their souls with us—"literally."

URSULA K. LEGUIN

The greatest thing in style is to have command of metaphor.

ARISTOTLE

When we come across a natural style, we are surprised and delighted, for we expected an author, and we find a man.

BLAISE PASCAL

The approach to style is by way of plainness, simplicity, orderliness, sincerity.

E.B. WHITE

Steady labor with the hands, which engrosses the attention also, is unquestionably the best method of removing palaver and sentimentality out of one's own style, both of speaking and writing. If [a man] has worked hard from morning till night, though he may have grieved that he could not be watching the train of his thought during that time, yet the few hasty lines which at evening record his day's experience will be more musical and true than his freest but idle fancy could have furnished.

HENRY DAVID THOREAU

When I sit down to write a book, I do not say to myself, "I am going to produce a work of art." I write it because there is some lie that I want to expose, some fact to which I want to draw attention, and my initial concern is to get a hearing.

GEORGE ORWELL

The style of the Bible...can be parodied but never duplicated. The elements that make the Bible the most expressive book in the world include concreteness, realism, simplicity, an elemental quality, brevity, repetition, emphasis on the spoken word, and affective power.

LELAND RYKEN

He who has nothing to say has no style and never will have style.

GEORGE BERNARD SHAW

Ultimately, eloquence...moves us with what it leaves unsaid, touching off echoes in what we already know from our reading, our religion and our heritage.

WILLIAM ZINSSER

If any man wish to write in a clear style, let him be first clear in his thoughts; and if any would write in a noble style, let him first possess a noble soul.

JOHANN WOLFGANG VON GOETHE

Learn as much by writing as by reading.

LORD ACTON

A book cannot be what a writer is not. Who you are informs how you write at the deepest level.

ANONYMOUS

The most important thing about having to read an essay aloud regularly is that it forces the undergraduate to write for reading aloud. Because he himself has to do the reading aloud, he soon becomes aware that he must make punctuational allowances for breathing pauses, which is the best way (because it is the most rudimentary way) to come to an understanding of sentence structure. The undergraduate must write so that when he reads aloud his tutor will understand without being obliged to request the repetition of a sentence or a phrase. It is understood that a request for the repetition of a passage is fatal.

GEORGE BAILEY

Lewis would always use analogy—the metaphor of syllogistic harness—to solve all problems. He did this sort of thing instinctively; it was his method of "picture thinking" which he used so extensively in his books.

GEORGE BAILEY

...English Style, familiar but not coarse, elegant, but not ostentatious...

SAMUEL JOHNSON

Have something to say, and say it as clearly as you can. That is the only secret of style.

MATTHEW ARNOLD

The great enemy of clear language is insincerity.

GEORGE ORWELL

If he would inform, he must advance regularly from Things known to things unknown, distinctly, without Confusion, and the lower he begins the better. It is a common Fault in Writers, to allow their Readers too much knowledge: They begin with that which should be the Middle, and skipping backwards and forwards, 'tis impossible for any one but he who is perfect in the Subject before, to understand their Work, and such an one has no Occasion to read it.

BENJAMIN FRANKLIN

The two capital secrets in the art of prose composition are these: first, the philosophy of transition and connection; or the art by which one step in an evolution of thought is made to arise out of another: all fluent and effective composition depends on the connections; secondly, the way in which sentences are made to modify each other; for the most powerful effects in written eloquence arise out of this reverberation, as it were, from each other in a rapid succession of sentences.

THOMA DE QUINCEY

There are two sorts of eloquence; the one indeed scarce deserves the name of it, which consists chiefly in laboured and polished periods an over-curious and artificial arrangements of figures, tinseled over with a gaudy embellishment of words…The other sort of eloquence is quite the reverse to this, and which may be said to be the true characteristic of the holy Scriptures; where the eloquence does not arise from a laboured and farfetched elocution, but from a surprising mixture of simplicity and majesty.

LAURENCE STERNE

A prudent man concealeth knowledge.

PROVERBS 12:23

My style of writing is chiefly grounded upon an early enthusiasm for Huxley, the greatest of all masters of orderly exposition. He taught me the importance of giving to every argument a simple structure.

                 H.L. MENKEN

The most emphatic place in clause or sentence is the end. This is the climax; and, during the momentary pause that follows, the last word continues, as it were to reverberate in the reader's mind. It has, in fact, the last word. One should therefore think twice about what one puts at a sentence-end.

                  F.L. LUCAS

Good prose is *direct, definite.* Like a firm handshake, it betokens confidence—and it inspires confidence. It implies to the reader: "You're in good hands with me. I have carefully thought out what I think about this subject and believe it makes sense, so I'm giving it to you just as I see it. I respect you too much to waste your valuable time with vagueness and wordiness, and I respect myself too much to be tempted into pussyfooting. Of course we'll probably disagree with one another here and there, but at least we'll both have the satisfaction of knowing precisely where we disagree.

                JOHN R. TRIMBLE

Carefully examined, a good—and interesting—style will be found to consist in a constant succession of tiny, unobservable surprises.

                FORD MADOX FORD

{8}

Simplicity

Simplicity is the mean between ostentation and rusticity.
ALEXANDER POPE

Perfect simplicity is unconsciously audacious.
GEORGE MEREDITH

Keep your paragraphs short, especially if you're writing for a newspaper or a magazine…Short paragraphs put air around what you write and make it look inviting, where one long chunk of type can discourage the reader from even starting to read.
WILLIAM ZINSSER

Use short sentences. Use short first paragraphs. Use vigorous English. Be positive, not negative. Eliminate every superfluous word. Avoid the use of adjectives, especially such extravagant ones as *splendid, gorgeous, grand, magnificent,* etc.
KANSAS CITY STAR STYLE SHEET

Fighting clutter is like fighting weeds—the writer is always slightly behind.

WILLIAM ZINSSER

Nowadays even if you could write a prose like Traherne's, you wouldn't be allowed to, for the canon of "functionalism" has disabled literature for half its functions.

C.S. LEWIS, PREFACE TO THE *SCREWTAPE LETTERS*

Vigorous writing is concise.

WILLIAM STRUNK JR.

In writing for publication the key word is style, and the key to good style is simplicity.

KENNETH HENSON

I want to give the audience a hint of a scene. No more than that. Give them too much and they won't contribute anything themselves. Give them just a suggestion and you get them working with you. That's what gives the theater meaning: when it becomes a social act.

ORSON WELLES

All your clear and pleasing sentences will fall apart if you don't keep remembering that writing is linear and sequential, that logic is the glue that holds it together, that tension must be maintained from one sentence to the next and from one paragraph to the next and from one section to the next, and that narrative—good old-fashioned storytelling—is what should pull your readers along without them noticing the tug.

WILLIAM ZINSSER

Often I think writing is sheer paring away of oneself leaving always something thinner, barer, more meager.
F. SCOTT FITZGERALD

The structure of every sentence is a lesson in logic.
JOHN STUART MILL

Sentences in their variety run from simplicity to complexity, a progression not necessarily reflected in length: a long sentence may be extremely simple in construction—indeed must be simple if it is to convey its sense easily.
SIR HERBERT READ

The problem well put is half solved.
JOHN DEWEY

The ability to simplify means to eliminate the unnecessary so that the necessary may speak.
HANS HOFMANN

Say all you have to say in the fewest possible words, or your reader will be sure to skip them; and in the plainest possible words or he will certainly misunderstand them.
JOHN RUSKIN

The indispensable characteristic of a good writer is a style marked by lucidity.
ERNEST HEMINGWAY

And how is clarity to be achieved? Mainly by taking trouble; and by writing to serve people rather than to impress them.
F.L. LUCAS

In 1942, Roosevelt's government came up with the following blackout order:

> Such preparations shall be made as will completely obscure all Federal buildings and non-Federal buildings occupied by the Federal government during an air raid for any period of time from visibility by reason of internal or external illumination.

Upon reading the memo, Roosevelt offered this edit: "Tell them that in buildings where they have to keep the work going to put something across the windows."

FROM ZINSSER'S *ON WRITING WELL*

1. Use subjects to name the characters of your story. [In other words, make the subject of your sentence the thing that carries out a specific action within the sentence.]

2. Use verbs to name important actions. [In other words, don't write, "The cause of our schools' failure at teaching basic skills is…" but "Our schools have failed to teach basic skills because…"]

3. Open your sentences with familiar units of information.

4. Get to the main verb quickly. [How?] Avoid long introductory phrases and clauses; avoid long abstract subjects; avoid interrupting the subject-verb connection.

5. Push new, complex units of information to the end of the sentence.

JOSEPH WILLIAMS IN *TEN LESSONS IN CLARITY AND GRACE*

{9}

Language

The words of the wise are as goads, and as nails fastened by the masters of assemblies, which are given from one shepherd.
ECCLESIASTES 12:11

Always be a poet, even in prose.
CHARLES PIERRE BAUDELAIRE

I like to write a column, then go back and check each and every verb. Is there a more vivid one to use? Should a man mull instead of think? Should he amble instead of walk? Should the parent rue instead of regret. Rue is somehow stronger. More Old Testament.
RHETA GRIMSLY JOHNSON

A simile may be compared to lines converging at a point, and is more excellent as the lines approach from a greater distance.
SAMUEL JOHNSON

Metaphors and similes can in unpracticed hands cause substantial damage to structures of meaning, somewhat like power tools misused by the unskilled.

JOHN MURRAY

Use similes sparingly. The simile is a common device and a useful one, but similes coming in rapid fire, one right on top of another, are more distracting than illuminating.

WILLIAM STRUNK JR. AND E.B. WHITE

The simile must be as precise as a slide rule and as natural as the smell of dill.

ISAAK BABEL

In all pointed sentences, some degree of accuracy must be sacrificed to conciseness.

SAMUEL JOHNSON

C.S. Lewis's mind was so highly developed that all of his arguments are illustrations while all of his illustrations are arguments.

J.I. PACKER

The difference between the right word and the nearly right word is the same as that between lightning and the lightning bug.

MARK TWAIN

Never use a long word when a diminutive one will do.

WILLIAM SAFIRE'S *FUMBLERULES*

Be sure you know the meaning (or meanings) of every word you use.

C.S. Lewis

It is well to remember that grammar is common speech formulated.
W. Somerset Maugham

English usage is sometimes more than mere taste, judgment, and education—sometimes it's sheer luck, like getting across a street.
E.B. White

You can be a little ungrammatical if you come from the right part of the country.
Robert Frost

Think about the words you use; be sure of their meanings. Get a usage manual and learn to identify such farcical words as *exemplarary*, *misunderestimate*, and *irregardless*.
T. Hensley

Prose alliteration should be used only for a special reason; when used by accident it falls upon the ear very disagreeably.
W. Somerset Maugham

When you've been standing before the Almighty, kings don't matter much, and big potentates are just small potatoes.
Vance Havner

I figured he was customer who had come to buy a rose bush and a bag of manure and be on his way.
T. Hensley

Tell it straight. Hemingway practiced eliminating adjectives. If you can do that and still make it interesting, your prose will be vigorous.

ELISABETH ELLIOT

The adjective is the banana peel of the parts of speech.

CLIFTON FADIMAN

Nice writing isn't enough. It isn't enough to have smooth and pretty language. You have to surprise the reader frequently, you can't just be nice all the time. Provoke the reader. Astonish the reader. Writing that has no surprises is as bland as oatmeal. Surprise the reader with the unexpected verb or adjective. Use one startling adjective per page.

ANNE BERNAYS

Don't say it was "delightful"; make us say "delightful" when we've read your description. You see, all those words (*horrifying, wonderful, hideous, exquisite*) are only like saying to your readers "Please will you do my job for me?"

C.S. LEWIS

Only presidents, editors and people with tapeworm have the right to use the editorial "we."

MARK TWAIN

When you refer back to a noun, repeat the noun or use a pronoun. Don't use "elegant variation." Don't refer to what you wrote or are going to write, but to what you talked about or are going to talk about. Don't use such words as *above*, *below*, or *hereafter*; instead, say *earlier, later, from now on*.

RUDOLPH FLESCH

When *whom* is correct recast the sentence.

WILLIAM SAFIRE

Rule of thumb: If the qualifying [clause] is set off by commas, use which; if not, use that.

JAMES J. KILPATRICK.

Never use slang except in dialogue and then only when unavoidable. Because all slang goes sour in a short time.

ERNEST HEMINGWAY

Avoid all prepositions and conjunctions that consist of more than one word. Aside from *inasmuch as*, this includes *with regard to, in association with, in connection with, with respect to, in the absence of, with a view to, in an effort to, in terms of, in order to, for the purpose of, for the reason that, in accordance with, in the neighborhood of, on the basis of*, and so on. There's not a single one of these word combinations that can't be replaced by a simple word like *if, for, to, by, about* or *since*.

RUDOLPH FLESCH

Learn punctuation; it is your little drum set, one of the few tools you have to signal the reader where the beats and emphases go. (If you get it wrong, any least thing, the editor will throw your manuscript out.) Punctuation is not like musical notation; it doesn't indicate the length of pauses, but instead signifies logical relations.

There are all sorts of people out there who know these things very well. You have to be among them even to begin.

ANNIE DILLARD

Cut out all those exclamation marks. An exclamation mark is like laughing at your own joke.

F. SCOTT FITZGERALD

Last but not least, avoid clichés like the plague.

WILLIAM SAFIRE'S *FUMBLERULES*

Don't use words too big for the subject. Don't say 'infinitely' when you mean 'very'; otherwise you'll have no word left when you want to talk about something really infinite.

C.S. LEWIS

Any word you have to hunt for in a thesaurus is the wrong word. There are no exceptions to this rule.

STEPHEN KING

Is every word doing new work? Can any thought be expressed with more economy? Is anything pompous or pretentious or faddish? Are you hanging on to something useless just because you think it's beautiful?

WILLIAM ZINSSER

I am not so lost in lexicography as to forget that words are the daughters of earth, and that things are the sons of heaven.

SAMUEL JOHNSON

To describe the act of love in detail without resorting to allegory, one is restricted to three choices: the language of the nursery, the language of the gutter, or the language of science—all are equally unsatisfactory.

C.S. Lewis

There are some punctuations that are interesting and there are some that are not.

Gertrude Stein

Good communication is half rational analysis and half pictorial and dramatic imagination, as in Isaiah and Ecclesiastes and Jesus and Paul and Luther and C.S. Lewis.

J.I. Packer

No idiom is taboo, no accent forbidden; there is simply a better chance of doing well if the writer holds a steady course, enters the stream of English quietly, and does not thrash about.

E.B. White

Don't use clichés, qualifiers, platitudes or overdone words.

Judy Delton

A book should consist of examples.

Wittgenstein

Detail makes the difference between boring and terrific writing. It's the difference between a pencil sketch and a lush oil painting. As a writer, words are your paint. Use all the colors.

Rhys Alexander

The great enemy of clear language is insincerity. When there is a gap between one's real and one's declared aims, one turns, as it

were instinctively, to long words and exhausted idiom, like a cuttlefish squirting out ink.
>
> GEORGE ORWELL

Why the copious flow of lachrymal fluid, my garrulous canine?
>
> DAFFY DUCK

{10}

Beginnings

Unless I have my first phrase, or first sentence, the rest doesn't follow.

RHETA GRIMSLY JOHNSON

One of the most difficult things is the first paragraph. I have spent many months on a first paragraph and once I get it, the rest just comes out very easily. In the first paragraph you solve most of the problems in your book. The theme is defined, the style, the tone. At least in my case, the first paragraph is a kind of sample of what the rest of the book is going to be.

GABRIEL GARCIA MARQUEZ

A bad beginning makes a bad ending.

EURIPIDES

The last thing one settles in writing a book is what one should put in first.

BLAISE PASCAL

If you take up Dr. Guthrie's sermons, you will find that he begins a thousand miles away from his text, apparently, and you wonder how he is ever going to get back to his theme.

D.L. MOODY

Begin every story in the middle. The reader doesn't care how it begins, he wants to get on with it.

LOUIS L'AMOUR

Make your characters want something right away even if it's only a glass of water. Characters paralyzed by the meaninglessness of modern life still have to drink water from time to time.

KURT VONNEGUT

Inspiration is wonderful when it happens, but the writer must develop an approach for the rest of the time...The wait is simply too long.

LEONARD BERNSTEIN (1918 - 1990)

Writing comes more easily if you have something to say.

SHOLEM ASCH

Good titles are critical because they are your first chance to hook readers.

KENNETH HENSON

What gets my interest is the sense that a writer is speaking honestly and fully of what he knows well.

WENDELL BERRY

It is in the hard, hard rock-pile labor of seeking to win, hold, or deserve a reader's interests that the pleasant agony of writing again comes in.

JOHN MASON BROWN

In an era of extremes, is there any room for understatement? In the realm of nonfiction, I'd like to argue that the answer is an understated "yes." Indeed, it's precisely when writing about subjects that seem extreme that understatement can be most effective. If your subject is grand or overwrought or hyperbolic, if it comes already laden with innate drama (real or manufactured), you might find that speaking softly works better than a big stick.

DAVID A. FRYXELL IN THE ESSAY, "QUIT SHOUTING!"

Endings

Nothing is more effective in giving the reader a sense that the subject has been covered than a return to a theme introduced in the lead.

Don McKinney

I always try to end sooner than the reader expects me to…The perfect ending should take the reader slightly by surprise and yet seem exactly right to him.

William Zinsser

The ending is where the reader discovers whether he has been reading the same story the writer thought he was writing.

John Updike

A good last sentence—or paragraph—is a joy in itself. It has its own virtues, which give the reader a lift and which linger when the article is over.

William Zinsser

A poem begins in delight and ends in wisdom; it inclines to the impulse, it assumes direction with the first line laid down, it runs a course of lucky events, and ends in a clarification of life—not necessarily a great clarification, such as sects and cults are founded on, but in a momentary stay against confusion.

ROBERT FROST

At least half the mystery novels published violate the law that the solution, once revealed, must seem to be inevitable.

RAYMOND CHANDLER

{12}

Revision

When you become hopelessly mired in a sentence, it is best to start fresh; do not try to fight your way through against the terrible odds of syntax. Usually what is wrong is that the construction has become too involved at some point; the sentence needs to be broken apart and replaced by two or more shorter sentences.

E.B. WHITE

Read over your compositions and, when you meet a passage which you think is particularly fine, strike it out.

SAMUEL JOHNSON

This morning I took the hyphen out of Hell-bound, and this afternoon I put it back in.

ATTRIBUTED TO EDWIN ARLINGTON ROBINSON

No writer's style just "happens," at least not in the first draft. If you have the luxury of time, let a piece simmer; take a walk, and when you return, it's as if somebody highlighted the weak phrases for you.

RHETA GRIMSLY JOHNSON

I write every paragraph four times: once to get my meaning down, once to put in everything I left out, once to take out everything that seems unnecessary, and once to make the whole thing sound as if I had only just thought of it.

ADOLPH MURIE

Delete every word that has no real work to do.

ELISABETH ELLIOT

When I am writing a column, I probably take out the words *really*, *actually*, and *very* more than any three other words. Those three words will appear in virtually every sentence in the rough draft.

DAVE BARRY

When you say something, make sure you have said it. The chances of your having said it are only fair.

E. B. WHITE

I try to leave out the parts that people skip.

ELMORE LEONARD

When you give up a bit of work don't (unless it is hopelessly bad) throw it away. Put it in a drawer. It may come in useful later. Much of my best work or what I think my best, is the rewriting of things begun and abandoned years earlier.

C.S. LEWIS

Proofread carefully to see if you any words out.
WILLIAM SAFIRE'S *FUMBLERULES*

I have made this [letter] longer, because I have not had the time to make it shorter.
BLAISE PASCAL, "LETTRES PROVINCIALES"

I was working on the proof of one of my poems all the morning, and took out a comma. In the afternoon I put it back again.
OSCAR WILDE

Many books require no thought from those who read them, and for a very simple reason; they made no such demand upon those who wrote them.
CHARLES CALEB COLTON

I believe more in the scissors than I do in the pencil.
TRUMAN CAPOTE

I turn sentences around. That's my life. I write a sentence and I turn it around. Then I look at it and I turn it around again. Then I have lunch. Then I come back in and write another sentence. Then I have tea and turn the new sentence around. Then I read the two sentences over and turn them both around. Then I lie down on my sofa and think. Then I get up and throw them out and start from the beginning.
PHILLIP ROTH

The most common pleasant thing people say to me about my writing is that it looks "effortless." [But] it is the opposite of effortless...I probably do 20 drafts of each chapter. I write something over and over. It's like *Groundhog Day*. My writing process is sweaty and inelegant.

MICHAEL LEWIS

You become a good writer just as you become a good joiner: by planning down your sentences.

ANATOLE FRANCE

I am unlikely to trust a sentence that comes easily.

WILLIAM GASS

The uncreative mind can spot wrong answers, but it takes a creative mind to spot wrong questions.

ANTONY JAY

What is written without effort is in general read without pleasure.

SAMUEL JOHNSON

Writing is transitions—which may be likened to stepping stones laid across a stream. If the distance between them is too great, the reader gets wet; if it is too short, the journey becomes boring.

T. HENSLEY

Writing and rewriting are a constant search for what it is one is saying.

JOHN UPDIKE

I am certainly no calligrapher, but my handwritten pages have a homemade, handmade look to them that both pleases me in itself and suggests the possibility of ready correction. It looks hospitable to improvement. As the longhand is transformed into typeset and then to galley proofs and the printed page, it seems increasingly to resist improvement…I have the notion…again unprovable—that the longer I keep a piece of work in longhand, the better it will be.

WENDELL BERRY

{13}

Editors

If your story comes back with a rejection note, don't take it personally or stew about it. Get it in the mail to another market that same day. (Then you can go back to whatever it is you were doing, preferably writing the next story.)

JEFFREY CARVER

What a good editor brings to a piece of writing is an objective eye that the writer has long since lost, and there is no end of ways in which an editor can improve a manuscript...[Whereas] a bad editor has a compulsion to tinker, proving with busywork that he hasn't forgotten the minutiae of grammar and usage.

WILLIAM ZINSSER

The truth is, an editor doesn't always think a raw manuscript is worth very much. What attracts an editor to it in the selection process often is its potential for being shaped into a successful product for the audience.

ARTHUR PLOTNIC

Editors specialize in knowing the audience. They live with it week to week; they ponder reader correspondence; they analyze the groups and subgroups making up the readership; and they study the spectrum of success and failure among media serving this audience. Because an editor's self-esteem and very job depend on satisfying the reader, it is the reader, not the author, who will receive first consideration when conflicts of interest arise.
ARTHUR PLOTNIC

Most writers won't argue with an editor because they don't want to annoy him; they're so grateful to be published that they agree to having their style—in other words, their personality—violated in public.
WILLIAM ZINSSER

No passion in the world is equal to the passion to alter someone else's draft.
H. G. WELLS (1866 - 1946)

A good many young writers make the mistake of enclosing a stamped, self-addressed envelope, big enough for the manuscript to come back in. This is too much of a temptation to the editor.
RING LARDNER, "HOW TO WRITE SHORT STORIES"

Some editors are failed writers, but so are most writers.
T. S. ELIOT

She signed only her initials, "B.C." Nowhere in the book [*My Utmost For His Highest*] did it mention her name or her work or taking shorthand notes, typing the talks, and merging paragraphs from three different messages into a coherent reading for a single

day. The author was Oswald Chambers. She was a channel through which his words were conveyed to others. That was her way.
>   DAVID MCCASLAND ON GERTRUDE CHAMBERS

Money

Sir, no man but a blockhead ever wrote except for money.
SAMUEL JOHNSON

I never had any doubts about my abilities. I knew I could write. I just had to figure out how to eat while doing this.
CORMAC MCCARTHY

All writers, no matter their prestige, are subject to the whims and malice of publishers' bookkeepers balancing their books by withholding the writers' fees: six months in arrears is the usual "float."
SOPHY BURNUM

Writers are vulnerable enough without being put through the repeated indignities of calling to learn the status of their article and to beg for money.
WILLIAM ZINSSER

Money, money, all is money! Could you write even a penny novelette without money to put heart in you?

GEORGE ORWELL

Writing is the only profession where no one considers you ridiculous if you earn no money.

JULES RENARD

{15}

The Writing Life

It turns out that writing a good query letter is one of the keys to getting published. The goal is to showcase your best writing while crassly pitching your story. I learned to write queries by looking at examples of them in Shirley's Biagi's, *How to Write & Sell Magazine Articles* and Don McKinney's *Magazine Writing That Sells*. These books helped me see the editor's plight: he is always up against a deadline, and terribly overworked. What he wants more than anything are writers who straight to the point.

T. HENSLEY

Try to be one of those people on whom nothing is lost.

HENRY JAMES

It takes audacity to be a writer—you have to believe without wavering that others need to hear what you have to say.

ANONYMOUS

A writer is something you are, whereas "author" refers to something you do. Almost anyone can be an author, from anthologists to autobiographers, diet doctors to financial gurus. Authors are a dime a dozen. Writers are rare.

JOHN WINOKUR

The writer's psychology is by its very nature one of extreme duality. The writer labors in isolation, yet all that intensive, lonely, work is in the service of community, is an attempt to reach another person.

BETSY LERNER

It's nervous work. The state you need to write in is the same state that others are paying large sums to get rid of.

SHIRLEY HAZZARD

The writer's life seethes within but not without.

ANTHONY BURGESS

Many writers are agnostic and have as their religion art, but just as many are conscious that the source of their gifts is God and have found thanksgiving, worship, and praise of the Holy Being to be central to their lives and artistic practice.

RON HANSEN

Every writer works at espionage, taking notes, observing particulars that everyone else overlooks, scouring the world for clues of meaning.

PHILLIP YANCEY

The relationship between journalist and subject is often an unspoken conspiracy.

DENNIS COVINGTON

The first four months of writing the book, my mental image is scratching with my hands through granite. My other image is pushing a train up a mountain, and it's icy, and I'm in bare feet.
MARY HIGGINS CLARK

A guest at a dinner party observed the strange expression on James Thurber's face. "Don't be concerned, said Thurber's wife. "He's writing."
SOPHY BURNHAM

The best part about writing is stopping.
COLIN WALTERS

The essayist is a self-liberated man, sustained by the childish belief that everything he thinks about, everything that happens to him is of general interest.
E.B. WHITE

What is a poet? A poet is an unhappy being whose heart is torn by secret sufferings, but whose lips are so strangely formed that when the sighs and the cries escape them, they sound like beautiful music.
SOREN KIERKEGAARD

Writing not only gives form and meaning to our sometimes disorderly existence, but gives the author the chance for self-disclosure and communion with others, while giving readers a privileged share in another's inner life that, perhaps imperceptibly, questions and illumines their own.
RON HANSEN

An essayist is a lucky person who has found a way to discourse without being interrupted.

CHARLES POORE

Those who have never carried a book through the press can form no idea of the amount of toil it involves. The process has increased my respect for authors a thousand fold. I think I would rather cross the African continent again than to undertake to write another book.

DAVID LIVINGSTONE

For several days after my first book was published I carried it about in my pocket, and took surreptitious peeks at in to make sure the ink had not faded.

J.M. BARRIE

I was in my twenties when I'd won the Pulitzer—I didn't mean to, it was an accident, these things just fall down on your head. I was horribly embarrassed and hid myself as far as I could.

ANNIE DILLARD

Unprovided with original learning, unformed in the habits of thinking, unskilled in the arts of composition, I resolved to write a book.

EDWARD GIBBON

I write entirely to find out what I'm thinking, what I'm looking at, what I see and what it means. What I want and what I fear.

JOAN DIDION

Literature is an occupation in which you have to keep proving your talent to people who have none.

JULES RENARD

The only reason for being a professional writer is that you can't help it.

LEO ROSTEN

I love being a writer. What I can't stand is the paperwork.

PETER DE VRIES

There is nothing to write about, you say. Well then, write and let me know just this—that there is nothing to write about; or tell me in the good old style if you are well. That's right. *I am quite well.*

PLINY THE YOUNGER, *LETTERS*

You have to know how to accept rejection and reject acceptance.

RAY BRADBURY

I write because I'm afraid to say some things out loud.

REALLIVEPREACHER.COM

If you want to write you must have faith in yourself. Faith enough to believe that if a thing is true about you, it is likely true about many people. And if you can have faith in your integrity and your motives, then you can write about yourself without fear.

REA LIVEPREACHER.COM

It took me fifteen years to discover that I had no talent for writing, but I couldn't give it up because by that time I was too famous.

ROBERT BENCHLEY

Every journalist has a novel in him, which is an excellent place for it.

RUSSEL LYNES

A writer is a person for whom writing is more difficult than it is for other people.

THOMAS MANN

If you want to be remembered well after you pass away, either write things worth reading or do things worth writing about.

BENJAMIN FRANKLIN

Writing is a dreadful labor, yet not so dreadful as idleness.

THOMAS CARLYLE

Telling a writer to relax is like telling a man to relax while being examined for a hernia.

WILLIAM ZINSSER

If they won't write the kind of books we want to read, we shall have to write them ourselves; but it is very laborious.

C.S. LEWIS TO J.R.R. TOLKIEN

The Christian writer does not decide what would be good for the world and proceed to deliver it. Like a very doubtful Jacob, he confronts what stands in his path and wonders if he will come out of the struggle at all.

FLANNERY O'CONNOR

Our response to life is different if we have been taught only a definition of faith than if we have trembled with Abraham as he held a knife over Isaac.

Flannery O'Connor

When I became a man, I put away childish things, including the fear of childishness and the desire to be very grown up.

C.S. Lewis

If you write for God, you will reach many men and bring them joy. If you write for men, you may make some money, and you may give someone a little joy, and you may make a noise in the world—for a little while. If you write only for yourself, you can read what you yourself have written, and after ten minutes, you will be so disgusted you will wish that you were dead.

Thomas Merton

A journalist's job is to comfort the afflicted and afflict the comfortable.

H.L. Mencken

Better to write for yourself and have no public, than to write for the public and have no self.

Cyril Connolly

Write something to suit yourself and many people will like it; write something to suit everybody and scarcely anyone will care for it.

Jesse Stuart

Read books. Not just good books. Great ones. Observe what it is that makes them interesting. We find ourselves mirrored in great literature. We experience the shock of recognition. "That's it! That's exactly what I felt/thought/meant/wanted to say!" Great books are "an axe to the frozen seas within us," Kafka said.

ELISABETH ELLIOT

For a first-time author, these are the best of times and the worst of times. Thanks to advances in self-publishing, anyone can get a book in print—as long as you're willing to bear the costs of production, marketing, and sales that used to be absorbed by publishers. Brick-and-mortar bookstores generally won't stock your book, so you have to find other ways to get the word out. Good luck.

PHILIP YANCEY

Writing *The Gambler* proved in every sense therapeutic. For financial reasons it had to be completed in twenty-six days, and to achieve this Dostoevsky procured the services of a stenographer, Anna Grigoryevna Snitkina, who turned out to be exceptionally competent and sensible, and in due course became his second and last wife.

MALCOLM MUGGERIDGE

Seven years, My lord, have now past since I waited in your outward Rooms or was repulsed from your Door, during which time I have been pushing on my work through difficulties of which it is useless to complain, and have brought it at last to the verge of Publication without one Act of assistance, one word of encouragement, or one smile of favour. Such treatment I did not expect, for I never had a Patron before... Is not a Patron, My Lord, one who looks with unconcern on a Man struggling for Life in the Water and when he has reached ground encumbers him with help? The notice which you have been pleased to take of my Labours, had it been early, had been kind; but it has been delayed till I am indifferent and cannot enjoy it, till I am solitary and cannot impart it, till I am known and do not want it.

SAMUEL JOHNSON, LETTER TO LORD CHESERFIELD

When I finished *The Boys of Summer*, in the spring of 1971, $380 remained in the family checking account. Our savings accounts, our stocks, and our weekend place in the Berkshires were history, all gone to fund this one, demanding book. With my enthusiastic support, my then-wife, in her second-finest hour, threw a glorious party. "I might as well celebrate," she said. "After all I've become the world's outstanding expert on Pee Wee Rese under the age of 30."

ROGER KAHN

I have found that the daily grind of business writing forces me to get to the point and to employ with some regularity a punchy metaphor that clinches the sale.

T. HENSLEY

By now, I suppose, I should count myself a professional, having published so much. But to myself I remain an amateur who scribbles till he likes his flow, then mails the result to the publisher (usually late), and moves on to the next thing so hastily that within 24 hours he forgets what he has written.

J.I. PACKER

The less conscious one is of being "a writer," the better the writing.

PICO IYER

I think all writing is a disease. You can't stop it.

WILLIAM CARLOS WILLIAMS

Writing is very hard work and knowing what you're doing the whole time.

SHELBY FOOTE

Writing is 90 percent procrastination: reading magazines, eating cereal out of the box, watching infomercials.

PAUL RUDNICK

Writing is like driving at night in the fog. You can only see as far as your headlights, but you can make the whole trip that way.

E.L. DOCTOROW

Good writing is always about things that are important to you, things that are scary to you, things that eat you up.

JOHN EDGAR WIDEMAN

All good writing is swimming under water and holding your breath.

F. SCOTT FITZGERALD

Writing is a combination of intangible creative fantasy and appallingly hard work.

ANTHONY POWELL

Writing is…that oddest of anomalies: an intimate letter to a stranger.

PICO IYER

Journalism is literature in a hurry.
                                    MATHEW ARNOLD

Critics and Criticism

The man who is asked by an author what he thinks of his work, is put to the torture, and is not obliged to speak the truth.
SAMUEL JOHNSON

People who like this sort of thing will find this the sort of thing they like.
ABRAHAM LINCOLN, REVIEWING A BOOK

Times are bad. Children no longer obey their parents, and everyone is writing a book.
CICERO

The multitude of books is a great evil. There is no measure or limit to this fever of writing; everyone must be an authority; some out of vanity to acquire celebrity; others for the sake of lucre and gain.
MARTIN LUTHER

This is not a novel to be tossed aside lightly. It should be thrown with great force.

DOROTHY PARKER

The rules governing literary art in the domain of romantic fiction...require that a tale shall accomplish something and arrive somewhere. But the *Deerslayer* tale accomplishes nothing and arrives in the air. . .[The rules] require [further] that the author shall make the reader feel a deep interest in the personages of his tale and in their fate; and that he shall make the reader love the good people in the tale and hate the bad ones. But the reader of the *Deerslayer* tale dislikes the good people in it, is indifferent to the others, and wishes they would all get drowned together.

MARK TWAIN, "FENNIMORE COOPER'S LITERARY OFFENSES"

Reading reviews of your own book is...a no-win game. If the review is flattering, one tends to feel vain and uneasy. If it is bad, one tends to feel exposed, found out. Neither feeling does you any good.

WALKER PERCY

Abuse is often of service: there is nothing so dangerous to an author as silence; his name, like a shuttlecock, must be beat backward and forward, or it falls to the ground...It is surely better a man should be abused than forgotten.

SAMUEL JOHNSON

In certain kinds of writing, particularly in art criticism and literary criticism, it is normal to come across long passages which are almost completely lacking in meaning.
>   GEORGE ORWELL, "POLITICS AND THE ENGLISH LANGUAGE"

In comparing various authors with one another, I have discovered that some of the gravest and latest writers have transcribed, word for word, from former works, without making acknowledgment.
>   PLINY THE ELDER, *NATURAL HISTORY*

If I read a book [and] it makes my whole body so cold no fire ever can warm me, I know that is poetry. If I feel physically as if the top of my head were taken off, I know that is poetry.
>   EMILY DICKINSON

Lewis had three standard forms of comment on an essay. If the essay was good: "There is a good deal in what you say." If the essay was middling: "There is something in what you say." If the essay was bad: "There may be something in what you say." His other fairly standard comments were: "Too much straw and not enough bricks," and, "Not with Brogans, please, slippers are in order when you proceed to make a literary point." Lewis was sparing of his compliments—the highest I know of was "Much of that was very well said"—but he was quick to notice any excellence of usage. He spent five minutes praising one word I had used to describe Dryden's poetry (the word 'bracing").
>   GEORGE BAILEY, AN AMERICAN STUDENT

Much literary criticism comes from people for whom extreme specialization is a cover for either grave cerebral inadequacy or terminal laziness, the latter being a much cherished aspect of academic freedom.

JOHN KENNETH GALBRAITH

Criticism may not be agreeable, but it is necessary. It fulfils the same function as pain in the human body. It calls attention to an unhealthy state of things.

WINSTON CHURCHILL

Don't mind criticism. If it is untrue, disregard it; if unfair, keep from irritation, if it is ignorant, smile; if it is justified, it is not criticism, learn from it.

ANONYMOUS

A Sample Query Letter

818 Cumberland Street
Bristol, VA 24201
(540) 466-2931 wk.
July 6, 2000

Toby Lester, Executive Editor
Country Journal
98 N. Washington Street
Boston, MA 02114

Dear Mr. Lester,

When my father was growing up in Southwest Virginia, farm power was mostly of the four-legged variety. Dad tells how, with a team of mules, he plowed a 10-acre field in the fourth grade.

I've always admired the feat—and wished I could make the same boast. But when I was coming up, horse farming was already a thing of the past. My only equine memory is of being led along on "Nancy," Dad's worn out mule.

But memories are like seeds. Given the right conditions, they sprout and grow. And that's exactly what happened several years ago when I stumbled on a copy of the *Small Farmer's Journal*, a quarterly dedicated to the promotion of sustainable agriculture in general, and horse farming in particular.

In reading the Journal, I discovered that there's a whole subculture of folks who still farm with horses. And not just that, there are schools and short courses for greenhorns like myself, who would like to know more about four-legged power, but aren't sure where to begin.

Which brings me to the reason for this letter. I would like to sign up for one of these courses, and then write about it for *Country Journal*. I'll learn how to plow with a No. 11 Oliver Sulky. Your readers will get to share the experience in article form.

I realize that the demographics of your readership might argue against such a piece. (Who's going to bother with horses these days, when tillers and tractors are so easy to keep?) Still, I suspect that even today's hybrid homesteader—whether he aspires to working with horses or not—will enjoy reading about my bruised toes and kicked shins. Add to that the smell of horse sweat and freshly turned earth, and I'm convinced this would be a memorable piece.

I'm thinking 3000 words, with a sidebar of horse course information and a glossary of draft horse terms. Title: "Gee, Haw, and What?: An Urban Homesteader Gets the Short Course in Four Legged Power."

Sound like material for Country Journal? I look forward to hearing from you soon.

       Sincerely,
       Tim Hensley

P.S. I have written for *Mother Earth News, Grit, Rural Living, Highlights for Children, Fine Gardening, Kitchen Gardener, and Smithsonian.* Clips enclosed.
P.P.S.[i] Thomas Fisher of *Horticulture* suggested that I contact you.

{18}

The Elements of Lincoln's Grammar

I am loath to close. We are not enemies, but friends. We must not be enemies. Though passion may have strained, it must not break our bonds of affection. The mystic chords of memory, stretching from every battlefield and patriot grave to every living heart and hearthstone all over this broad land, will yet swell the chorus of the Union, when again touched, as surely they will be, by the better angels of our nature.

—ABRAHAM LINCOLN

In a day when *redundancy* and *emotionalism* are the high water marks of communication excellence, the elegance and concision of Abraham Lincoln's prose style serves as a startling reminder of just how far our national discourse has sunk.

Lincoln is regarded as the best writer among our American presidents. His *Second Inaugural* is ranked among the greatest literature of all time. The *Gettysburg Address* has been described as the "perfect specimen of English composition."

How did a farm boy whose formal education lasted less than a year come to write such memorable and enduring prose?

*1. **Lincoln was a reader**.* Though the books available to him were few—most notably, *Aesop's Fables, Pilgrim's Progress,* Weems's *Washington, Robinson Crusoe,* and the King James Bible—Lincoln read and reread these works in such a way that their content and style became his own: the pathos of *Pilgrim's Progress,* the sense of destiny in Weems's *Washington,* the venerable phrasing of the King James Bible.

*2. **Lincoln was a lover of poetry**.* As a boy he wrote in the margin of his copy book: "Abraham Lincoln / His hand and pen / He will be good / But God knows when." As a young man Lincoln wrote poems about insanity, the creation of Eve, a visit to his mother's grave. When Lincoln came across the poem, "Oh! Why Should the Spirit of Mortals be Proud?" by William Knox, he said, "I would give all I am worth and go into debt, to be able to write so fine a piece as I think that is." Lincoln was always conscious of the poetic potential of words.

*3. **Lincoln studied grammar**.* While keeping store in Springfield, at the age twenty-one, he confided to his friend, Mentor Graham, "I've got a good notion to study grammar." Graham, a school teacher by trade, knew of a copy of *Kirkham's Grammar* at the home of a Mr. John C. Vaner six miles from Springfield. Lincoln got up from the breakfast table, walked the six miles to Vaner's house, and "soon returned to the store with the coveted volume under his arm. With zealous perseverance he at once applied himself to the book. Sometimes he would stretch out full length upon the store counter, his head propped up on a stack of calico prints, studying it."[ii] Years later, Lincoln commented on this period in his life: "After I had separated from my father, I studied English grammar, imperfectly of course, but so as to speak and write as well as I do now."

4. Lincoln's language was rooted in Anglo-Saxon. Some might regard this as an out-of-the-way point. But Anglo-Saxon is the language of our earliest associations: *father, mother, husband, brother, home* and *hearth.* It is simple and emotional and picturesque. In the head quote at the beginning of this essay, Lincoln says, "I am loathe to close." The Latin equivalent for *loathe* is *abhor* or *aver* or *detest.* The Greek equivalent: *antipathy.* "I feel a great *antipathy* toward closing?"—No, the simplicity of "I am loathe to close" works much better.

5. Lincoln employed a strict economy of language. The *Gettysburg Address* is 10 sentences long, a mere 272 words. Of these, 204 are one-syllable, 50 are two-syllable, 18 three syllables or more. But with these simple words Lincoln summed up in a two-minute speech, as no one ever had, the ideals of the American experiment, and the essential meaning of the Civil War. William Strunk says that "a sentence should contain no unnecessary words, a paragraph no unnecessary sentences, for the same reason that a drawing should have no unnecessary lines and a machine no unnecessary parts." Lincoln applied this principle with such skill that it is hard to read his work and not be struck by its forceful economy.

6. Lincoln balanced logic with anecdote and image. A self-taught surveyor and a student of Euclid's *Geometry*, Lincoln was gifted with a logical mind. His law partner, William Herndon, described him as a "deep and close thinker." But he always anchored his discourses in common experience, and in the imagery of the natural world. In the *Gettysburg Address,* for example, he writes that the United States was "conceived in liberty" and "brought forth" by our fathers—the imagery of birth. And what sort of nation was so conceived and born? A nation "dedicated to the proposition that all men are created equal"—a lofty, platonic ideal. Or again in the head quote above, an abstract plea: "We must not be enemies," followed by the image of "mystic chords of memory stretching from every battlefield and patriot grave to every living heart and hearthstone all over this broad land." In short, Lincoln was a master at weaving together abstract concepts and vivid metaphors.

7. **Lincoln revised his compositions tirelessly**. That is to say, he did not scribble the *Gettysburg Address* on a scrap of paper as he rode the train from Washington to Gettysburg. Rather, he began working on the address well in advance of the ceremony; he worked on it while he was in Gettysburg; he even inserted the phrase, "under God," extemporaneously.

Once Lincoln was asked how he was able to express himself with such simplicity. He explained that when he was a boy he would become upset when grown-ups spoke in a way that he could not understand, and that he would stay up at night, mulling over what he had heard, trying to put it in simpler terms: "I could not sleep when I got on such a hunt for an idea until I had caught it; and when I thought I had got it, I was not satisfied until I had repeated it over and over; until I had put it in language plain enough, as I thought, for any boy I knew to comprehend. This was a kind of passion with me and has stuck by me; for I am never easy now, when I am handling a thought, till I have bounded north and bounded it south, and bounded it east and bounded it west."

8. **Lincoln refused to compromise his integrity**. Perhaps the most notable example of this quality is his refusal at Cooper Union to leave off the remark, "A house divided against itself cannot stand." His friends told him that prophesying the dissolution of the Union in such plain terms would only stir up dissension. Lincoln held his course. He knew that these words from the lips of Jesus would resonate with the common man. And as it turned out, the speech at Cooper Union catapulted Lincoln into the national spotlight as an incisive thinker and a capable leader of men.[iii]

9. **Lincoln showed genuine humility**. The *Second Inaugural*, in particular, could have been Lincoln's victory paean. Delivered on March 4, 1865 with the end of the war in sight, it afforded Lincoln an opportunity to exult in successes of the Northern Army, and to excoriate the war mongering "miscreants" of the South. That is the term Henry Ward Beecher used in his victory speech at the reopening of Fort Sumter on April 14, 1865. "I charge the whole guilt of this war upon the ambitious, educated, plotting, political leaders of the South," he said "They have shed this ocean of blood."

But Lincoln's refused. He allowed instead that "offenses must come," and that it was God who gave "to both North and South this terrible war as the woe due to those by whom the offense came." And, if God deemed that the war "continue until all the wealth piled by the bondsman's two hundred and fifty years of unrequited toil shall be sunk, and until every drop of blood drawn with the lash shall be paid by another drawn with the sword, as was said three thousand years ago, so still it must be said 'the judgments of the Lord are true and righteous altogether.'"

*10. **Lincoln pondered the eternal**.* Why is one man more religious than another? It is not an easy question. In Lincoln's case, we know that he was no stranger to death. His mother died in 1818 when he was nine years old. His sister died giving birth in 1828. His first romantic interest, Ann Rutledge, died in 1835 at the age of 22. And he watched two of his own children succumb to childhood diseases: Eddie in 1850, a month before his fourth birthday, and Tad in 1862, at the age of eleven.

These experiences prompted in Lincoln a melancholy spirit so profound that it sometimes unnerved his associates. It was the sort of heaviness that people seek medication for today. But here was a prescription written by a sovereign God to bring to pass the spiritual rebirth of the great emancipator himself. Herndon always swore that Lincoln was a "completely secular" man—and indeed he worked this notion into his biography of the President. But after Lincoln gave the great speech at Gettysburg, he reportedly confided to a friend, "When I left Springfield I asked the people to pray for me. I was not a Christian. When I buried my son, the severest trial of my life, I was not a Christian. But when I went to Gettysburg and saw the graves of thousands of our soldiers, I then and there consecrated myself to Christ."

On Tuesday, April 13, 1865, Lincoln wrote a letter to the session of the New York Avenue Presbyterian Church in Washington where he regularly attended the Wednesday prayer meetings. He said that he had been considering his need to make a public confession of faith in Christ, and that he wished to do so the following Easter Sunday.

Sadly, that day never came for Lincoln; he was assassinated by John Wilkes Booth at Ford's Theater on the evening of Good Friday. Before daybreak the next morning, the great communicator had passed into eternity. "Now he belongs to the ages," said Stanton. He said, perhaps, more than he knew.

17 Figures of Speech

1. **Simile** – a comparison using like or as.
   - As the mountains are round about Jerusalem, so the Lord is round about his people, from henceforth even forever. (Ps. 124:2)
   - Life is like an isthmus between two eternities.
2. **Metaphor** – a direct comparison.
   - By a street called By-and-by you reach a house called Never.
   - Spare moments are the gold dust of time.
   - If you had not plowed with my heifer, you had not found out my riddle. —Sampson in the Bible
3. **Personification** – investing the inanimate (or nonhuman) with intelligence.
   - Leviathan counts darts as stubble; he laughs at the shaking of a spear. —Book of Job
   - The hungry flames.
   - The whistling wind.

- This tree invited me to sit in its shade.
- "Virginia Beauty and Her Kin"

4. **Apostrophe** – speaking aside to an idea, object or person not present.
    - O death, where is thy sting? O grave where is thy victory? (I Cor. 15:55)
    - Red bird, red bird, what do you see? Says, "I see a lone wolf looking back at me.

5. **Metonomy** – substitution.
    - He loves the bottle.
    - The kettle is boiling.

6. **Synecdoche** – a part represents the whole (or whole reps. part).
    - America won the Davis Cup.
    - All hands on deck!

7. **Hyperbole** – exaggeration, lit. *casting beyond*.
    - Rivers of waters run down my eyes because they keep not thy law. (Ps. 119)
    - I've been looking all over creation for you.
    - We laughed our heads off.
    - I've told you a million times.
    - If your right eye offends you, pluck it out.

8. **Understatement** – not head on, oblique; a literary flanking maneuver, surprising and often humorous. It assumes an intelligent, engaged reader.
    - "News of my recent death has been greatly exaggerated." —Mark Twain
    - "My impression is that the chief objection arises from the disordered condition of the hair." —A. Lincoln explaining

- why some of his acquaintances disliked a photo of him which captured his hair in an utterly disheveled condition.
- "To Alleviate Fears of Premature Burial" —Title of essay about the practices of embalmers.
- This plant requires very little water. –A garden worker's comment about an artificial, potted plant.
- "I took a walk along the historic coast of Normandy in the country of France. It was a lovely day for strolling along the seashore. Men were sleeping on the sand, some of them sleeping forever. Men were floating in the water, but they didn't know they were in the water, for they were dead." —Ernie Pyle

9. **Irony or Paradox** – reversal is employed. We mean the opposite of what we say. We ridicule the thing we praise.
   - "Here under leave of Brutus, and the rest (for Brutus is an honorable man; so are they all, all honorable men) come I to speak in Caesars's funeral. He was my friend, faithful and just to me: But Brutus says he was ambitious; And Brutus is an honorable man." —Shakespeare
   - a "A Modest Proposal" —Swift
   - Behold your king! —Pilate of Jesus
   - Forgive me this wrong. –Paul (I Cor. 12:13)

10. **Oxymoron** – contradictory things are paired. Lit. sharp/dull.
    - You got pain? Get the icy-hot patch.
    - If you lose your life, you'll save it.
    - When I am weak, then I am strong.

11. **Alliteration** – repetition of the same initial consonant.
    - Respect, Responsibility, Recreation, Romance.

- "Budget Woes Worsen."
- "Ventura Vetoes Plan."
- Davy smacked, swallowed, sank to yet more earnest sleep.

12. **Assonance** – the repetition of similar sounds in successive words.
    - "The rewards of the game are immeasurable: elegance, balance, beauty, simplicity—and perhaps most important, the fraternity of those who have tasted the mysteries of checkers." From "There is a Certain Amount of Humor in Checkers."

13. **Litotes** – a figure of emphasis, using a negative to create a positive.
    - Not half bad.
    - Luke in Acts: "Of men not a few," ref to Bereans; "Not a little comforted," when Eutychus revives; "Showed us "no little kindness," on Malta.

14. **Erotesis** – question. The figure employed most often by Jesus.
    - Who do men say that I am?
    - How do you read the scripture?
    - Art thou a master of Israel and knowest not these things?

15. **Synesthesia** – mixing or confusion of the senses.
    - She talked a blue streak.
    - I was seeing red.
    - I smelled the nine when I saw it, a putrid fishy smell that made me gag.

16. **Anaphora** – repetition of a word or phrase.

- "Scrooge was his sole executor, his sole administrator, his sole assignment, his sole residuary legatee, his sole friend and sole mourner." –Dickens
- "I lick the front page, which is all advertisements for films and dances in the city. I lick the headlines. I lick the great attacks of Patton and Montgomery in France and Germany. I lick the war in the Pacific. I lick the obituaries and the sad memorial poems, the sports pages, the market prices of eggs, butter and bacon. I suck the paper till there isn't a smidgen of grease." —Frank McCourt

17. **Onomatopoeia** – imitative sound inside a word.
    - "When bees buzz and cymbals clang, the reader's awareness is pricked. A slap is an onomatopoeia in and of itself, the word registering the accompanying sound. When characters or objects rattle, bang, screech, wheeze, fizz, zap, growl, roar, crackle or pop, the writer has reduced his need for description." —from *Writer's Digest*
    - "...but hearing Dad wrack and hawk and bits of his lung hitting whang in the pan..."

How many figures?
- "Oh! But he was a tight-fisted hand to the grindstone, Scrooge! A squeezing, wrenching, grasping, scraping, clutching, covetous old sinner! Hard and sharp as flint, from which no steel had ever struck out generous fire; secret, and self-contained and solitary as an oyster...He carried his own low temperature always about with him;

he iced his office in the dog-days; and didn't thaw it one degree at Christmas." —Dickens

The Anglo-Saxon Element

From *Lessons in English.* Ginn & Company, 1892, by Elisabeth Husted Lockwood

The Study of Etymology. — In order to use good English, we must know how to choose our words. To this end, we should learn to tell from the looks of a word whether it is really English or borrowed from some other tongue. We should know, too, just what the word means, so as to be able to use it in the right way. For this reason, we must learn the most important principles of Etymology, the science which treats of the derivation and meaning of words. An explanation of terms used in the science is given below, for the benefit of any who may not be familiar with them.

The Root of a Word. — When a word cannot be reduced to a simpler form in the language to which it belongs, it is called a root, a radical, or a primitive word. Ex. go, man.

Compound Words.—When a word is formed by uniting two or more simple words, it is called a compound word. Ex. butter-fly, rose-bud.

Derivative Words. — When a word is made by joining to a root either a prefix or a suffix, or both, it is called a derivative word.

A Prefix is a syllable or syllables placed before the root, to vary the meaning of the word; as, *il*-legal, not legal.

A Suffix is a syllable or syllables placed at the end of a root, to vary the meaning of the word; as, student one who studies.

An Affix is the general name, referring to a syllable fixed to the root. It is, therefore, applied to either a prefix or a suffix.

Two Great Elements of the Language.— The English language, as has been shown, is made up of words from many sources; but for convenience, it may be considered as containing two main elements:.—

1. The Anglo-Saxon, including words from other Teutonic tongues, such as the Danish.
2. The Classical, including the Latin and the Greek.

Importance of the Anglo-Saxon Element. — The Anglo-Saxon element is the more important, for two reasons: —

First. Because it is the native part of the language.

Second. Because it is the larger element in common use among English-speaking people.

Numerical Ratio of the Two Elements. — It has been shown in the preceding chapter that of the words in the dictionary, less than one-half are Saxon, nearly one-half Latin, and the remainder Greek and miscellaneous in origin. In common use, however, the number of Saxon words is relatively greater, because almost all the connecting words and the articles, pronouns, and auxiliary verbs are of Saxon origin, and these are used more frequently than any other words. It has been found by actual count that in the writings of about twenty good English authors, thirty-two words in forty are of Saxon origin. In Shakespeare and Milton, thirty-three words in forty are Saxon. The Bible is written in purer English than any other book which we have, some parts of it containing thirty-nine Saxon words in forty. How we may know Saxon Words. — Two things help us to determine whether a word is of Anglo-Saxon origin: first, the form of the word; second, the sense in which it is used. It must be borne in mind that there are exceptions to some of the rules which follow. For example, *un* is a Saxon prefix, but we find it in many words of Latin origin. In all doubtful cases, the pupil should consult the etymological dictionary.

Words distinguished as Saxon by their Form.

(a) Our Articles : a, an, the.

All Pronouns : we, this, which, etc.

All Auxiliary Verbs : have, may, will.

All Adjectives compared irregularly : good, bad, little.

Nearly all Irregular and Defective Verbs : am, go, ought.

Nearly all Prepositions and Conjunctions : and, with, by, as.

(b) Nearly all words which, in any of their forms, undergo vowel changes.

Adjectives with two comparisons : old, older, oldest. elder, eldest.

Adjectives changed to nouns : strong, strength.

Nouns changed to verbs : bliss, bless.

Nouns forming plurals by vowel change : foot, feet.

Verbs with strong preterites : fall, fell.

Verbs changed by form from intransitive to transitive : rise, raise.

(c) Most words of one syllable.

Parts of the body: head, ear, skull, (not face).

The senses : sight, touch, smell.

Infirmities : blind, lame, deaf.

The elements : fire, wind, frost, (not air).

Products : grass, corn, bread.

Fuel : coal, wood, peat.

Domestic animals : cat, dog, horse.

(d) All words beginning with wh, *kn*, *sh*: when, know, shine.

Most words beginning with *ea*, *ye*, *gl*, *th* : each, yearn, glad, thus.

Most words ending with *t*, *th*: beat, truth.

(e) Most compound and derivative words, the elements of which exist and have a meaning in English : horse back, shipwreck, winsome.

(f) Most words with Anglo-Saxon prefixes and suffixes.

ANGLO-SAXON PREFIXES.

1. **a-** = *in, on, at* (corruption of *on*).

a-bed, *in* bed. a-board, *on* board. a-back, *at* the back.

2. **be-** = *by*.

be-cause, *by* cause.

It is often intensive, as in be-stir, be-deck, be-come.

3. **for-** = *against, away*.

for-bid, to bid *against*, for-bear, to bear *away*.
for-give, formerly to give *away*.

4. **fore-** = *before*.
fore-tell, to tell *before*.

5. **mis-** = denotes wrong, evil.
mis-take, to take *wrongly*, mis-chance, *ill* chance.

6. **n-** = *not*.
n-ever, *not* ever.
n-either, *not* either.
n-one, *not* one.

7. **out-** = *beyond*.
out-law, *beyond* the law.

8. **over-** = *above*, or *beyond* the limit.
over-spread, to spread *above*
over-do, to do *too much*.

9. **to-** = (corruption of *the*).
to-day, *the* day. To-morrow, *the* morrow

10. **un-** = *not*.
un-truth, *not* the truth.
un-honored, *not* honored.

11. **under-** = *beneath*.

    under-go, to go *beneath*.

12. **up-** = *up*.

    up-hold, to hold *up*,

    up-land, up-start, up-right.

13. **with-** = against.

    with-stand, to stand *against*.

ANGLO-SAXON SUFFIXES.

Noun Suffixes = *one who* (agent).

    1. **-ar.** li-ar, *one who* lies.
    2. **-ard.** drunk-ard, *one who* drinks.
    3. **-er.** cri-er, *one who* cries.
    4. **-yer.** law-yer, *one who* understands law.
    5. **-ster.** young-ster, *one who* is young.

Noun Suffixes = *state, condition, quality*.

    6. **-dom.** king-dom, *state* of a king.
    7. **-ship.** friend-ship, *condition* of friends.
    8. **-hood.** man-hood, *state* of man.
    9. **-head.** god-head, same as god-hood.
    10. **-ness.** good-ness, *quality* of being good.

Noun Suffixes = *little*.

    11. **-ling.** dar-ling, a *little* dear.
    12. **-kin.** lamb-kin, a *little* lamb.

13. **-ie.** dog-gie, a *little* dog.
14. **-ock.** hill-ock, a *little* hill.
15. **-let.** stream-let, a *little* stream. (From the French.)
16. **-en.** chick-en, a *little* chick.

Adjective Suffixes = *like, having the quality of, relating to.*
17. **-ful.** cheer-ful, *having the quality of* cheer.
18. **-ly.** kingly, *like* a king.
19. **-ish.** boy-ish, *having the qualities of* a, boy.
    Engl-ish, *originating with* the Angles.
20. **-en.** wood-en, *having qualities of* wood.
21. **-ern.** north-em, *relating to* the north.
22. **-y.** gloom-y, *having the qualities of* gloom.
23. **-like.** god-like, *like* a god.

Miscellaneous Suffixes.
24. **-less** = *loss*, hope-less, with *loss* of hope.
25. **–some.** lone-some, hand-some.
26. **-teen** = ten. four-teen, four and *ten*.
27. **-ty** (from *tig*) = *decade*, for-ty, four *times ten*.
28. **-ward** = *towards*, east-ward, *towards* the east.
29. **-wise** = *manner*, like-wise, in like *manner*.
30. **-en.** Forms verbs from adjectives, weak, weaken. Plural nouns, ox-en, childr-en.

Words distinguished as Saxon by their Use and Meaning.
(a) Most of the words which we early learn to use, and which are most closely associated with the pleasant memories of

childhood and home. Such words have more power over us than have the high-sounding words which we learn later in life. Perhaps this is the reason why we find a simple Saxon style so pleasing.

Among the classes of Saxon words which we learn in childhood are the following : —

1. Names of our earliest and dearest associations.

    Ex. home, friends, father, mother, husband, wife, son, daughter, brother, sister, fireside, hearth.
2. Words expressing our strongest natural feelings.

    Ex. gladness (not *joy*), sorrow (not *grief*), tears, smiles, blushes, laughing, weeping, sighing, groaning, love, hate (not *anger*) , fear, pride, mirth.

    So also hungry, thirsty, tired, sleepy, lonesome, homesick, naughty.
3. Names of common things, such as a child early notices and learns to talk about.

    Ex. sun, moon, star, sky, cloud, earth, water.

    Animals : horse, cow, dog, cat, calf, pig (*beef, veal,* and *pork* are Norman terms).

    Objects in the plant world : tree, bush, grass (not *flower* or *vine*) .

    Objects in the mineral world : sand, salt, iron, gold, stone (not *rock*).

    Features of scenery : hill, woods, stream, land, sea (not *mountain* or *valley*)

Natural divisions of time, etc. : day, night, morn ing, evening, noon, midnight, sunset, sunrise, twilight, light, darkness.

Kinds of weather, etc. : cold, heat, wet, dry, wind, frost, hail, rain, sleet, snow, thunder, lightning, storm.

Parts of the body: hand, arm, head, leg, eye, ear, foot, nose (not *face*).

(b) Most of our particular terms. The general terms are mainly from the Latin, as will be seen from the following examples: —

Latin: motion, color, sound, animal, number.
Saxon: slide, creep, walk, fly, swim, etc.
   white, blue, red, green, yellow, etc.
   buzz, speak, whistle, roar, etc.
   animaL dog, man, sheep, wolf, etc.
   all the cardinal numbers to a million, and all the ordinal numbers except *second*.

This explains why the Saxon style is more vivid and pic turesque, and therefore more pleasing than a style which abounds in words of classic origin.

(c) Most of the words used in the common affairs of every day life.
 The words which we hear in the home, on the street, in the shops and markets, and on the farm are, to a great extent, Saxon words.

Ex. sell, buy, cheap, dear, high, low, weight (not *measure*), work, grind, reap, sow, baker, shoemaker, worth, want, wedge, spring, scrape, sweep, wash, rich, poor, business, wages (not *salary*).

Caution : Notice that many such words are not of Saxon origin. For example, *money*. In all doubtful cases consult the dictionary.

(d) Many colloquialisms ; that is, words which are used in familiar conversation. An excited talker does not stop to choose the most elegant word. When a man is angry, he " talks plain English," and uses such words as *lazy, shiftless, sly, gawky, shabby, trash, sham*.

(e) Most words in our proverbs and maxims.

These "old sayings," or "household words," as they are sometimes called, owe much of their force to their simple Saxon style.

Ex. "Make hay while the sun shines." "A bird in the hand is worth two in the bush." "No pains, no gains." "Look before you leap."

~ ~ ~

SAXON. —There was a little girl,
        And she had a little curl
        That hung right down on her forehead;
        And when she was good
        She was very, very good;

But when she was bad, she was horrid.

CLASSICAL. —At a recent period in the annals of the human family, there existed a diminutive feminine specimen of humanity, whose most conspicuous personal decoration was a capillary spiral appendage of minute dimensions. This descended perpendicularly upon her alabaster brow. At intervals when she was amiably disposed, she produced upon all beholders the impression of being excessively agreeable; but when she was amiably disposed, she produced upon all beholders the impression of being excessively agreeable; but when she abandoned herself to the natural inclinations of an unregenerate spirit, she exhibited such symptoms of depravity that her deportment became positively execrable.

~ ~ ~

SAXON. —A little boy once said to his mother, "Ma, if a bear should eat me up, where would my soul go?" She replied, "Your soul would go to Heaven, my son." He thought a minute, and then suddenly broke out, "If the bear should take to runnin', I'd have a good ride anyhow."

CLASSICAL. —A diminutive specimen of the human race propounded the following query to his maternal ancestor: "Mamma, if a carnivorous individual should devour me, whither would that ethereal portion of my human organization rejoicing in the euphonious appellation soul depart?" Mamma replied to her lineal descendant: "It would soar to the celestial regions." The youth cogitated for several consecutive moments, and then ejaculated, "If the animal should be seized with an unaccountable tendency to propel himself to a destination far remote, I should experience the delicious sensation of obtaining a glorious journey without being obliged to employ my powers of locomotion."

{21}

The Cumulative Sentence

There are three main types of sentences: the balanced sentence, the periodic sentence, and the cumulative sentence.

1. The **Balanced Sentence** is common in expositional writing and oratory. It facilitates comparison and contrast. The two halves of the sentence are divided by a semicolon or a dash.

> Ask not what your country can do for you—ask what you can do for your country.
> JOHN F. KENNEDY

> The inherent vice of capitalism is the unequal sharing of blessings; the inherent vice of socialism is the unequal sharing of mistakes.
> WINSTON CHURCHILL

2. The **Periodic** sentence is common in expositional writing as well. Its chief characteristics are a delayed verb and one or more

subordinate clauses (beginning usually with one of the "w words," *who, what, which, when,* etc.). The periodic sentence is *non-cumulative* in that its modifying elements are inter-dependent rather than additional.

> Those who are appalled by the prospect of living in a universe which, for the first time in several centuries, has ceased to seem comprehensible **may be** somewhat **reassured** by the reminder that it is only the novelty of the modern instances which is disturbing and that they have all along been living with other irresolvable paradoxes which did not trouble them simply because they had been so long accepted.
> JOSEPH WOOD KRUTCH

3. The **Cumulative** sentence is common in descriptive and narrative writing. It consists of a base clause (a subject and verb) with free or imbedded modifiers: *adjectives*, *adverbs*, and *phrases*. These modifiers take the place of subordinate clauses; they "accumulate" usually at the end of the sentence, adding layer upon layer of specific detail. They are the principal unit of the professional writer.[iv]

> It was a slaty, windy **day** with specs of snow sliding through the trees.
> SAUL BELLOW

She met him at the appointed time in the Plaza lobby, a lovely, faded, gray-eyed blonde.
                                              F. SCOTT FITZGERALD

The picadors **galloped** jerkily around the ring.
                                                ERNEST HEMINGWAY

We **caught** two bass, hauling them in briskly as though they were mackerel, pulling them over the side of the boat in a businesslike without any landing net and stunning them with a blow to the back of the head.
                                                          E.B. WHITE

Stretching away, **the cotton fields**, slowly emptying, were becoming the **color** of the sky, a deepening blue so intense that it was like darkness itself.
                                                       EUDORA WELTY

How grateful **they** had been for the coffee, she looking up at him, tremulous, her lips pecking at the cup, he blessing the coffee as it went down her.
                                                   HORTENSE CALISHER

Joad's lips stretched tight over his long teeth for a moment, and he **licked** his lips like a dog, two licks, one in each direction from the middle.
                                                         JOHN STEINBECK

Notes

[i] My copy of this letter gives "P.S.S." here rather than "P.P.S."—a glaring error. If I failed to correct this in the mailed copy, it's a wonder Mr. Lester didn't balk at the proposal. Perhaps he assumed that bad usage and horse farming go together.

[ii] Herndon, William. *Herndon's Lincoln.*

[iii] Some would argue that Lincoln's adherence to the principle of Union was a great mistake. Teacher and author, Dave Black, writes, for example, that "By destroying the right of secession, Lincoln and the Republican Party opened the floodgates to the unrestrained, despotic state the U.S. government has become today." I am of the opinion, however, that Lincoln's fight for the Union shows a firm adherence to a higher principle, namely that unity and righteousness are more important than autonomy.

[iv] All of these quotes are drawn from Bonniejean Christensen's book, *The Christensen Method,* which my professor at Southeastern College, L. Percival Breusch, used as the primary text in his essay course. The advice I remember most from Bro. Breusch was that our writing should be "thick and tight"—which admonition in itself is a pretty good definition of the cumulative sentence.

www.ingramcontent.com/pod-product-compliance
Lightning Source LLC
Chambersburg PA
CBHW031451040426
42444CB00007B/1052